Kidders Re[

An Eighteenth Century Recipe Book

With an Introduction and Glossary by
Jane Jakeman

ASHMOLEAN MUSEUM OXFORD

2001

EDW. KIDDER
Paſtry-maſter.

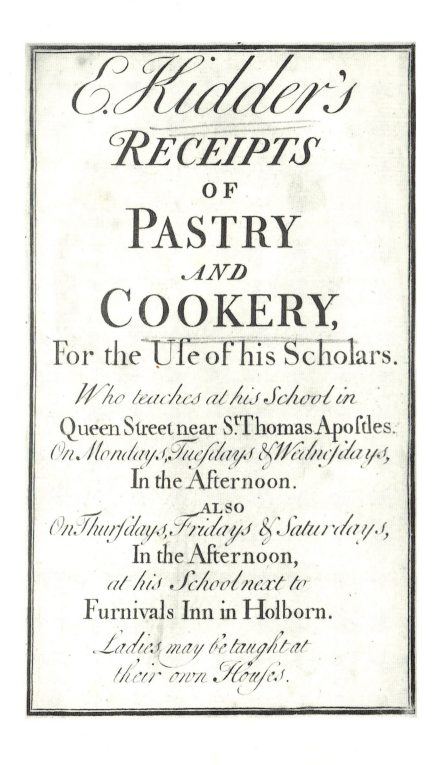

E. Kidder's
RECEIPTS
OF
PASTRY
AND
COOKERY,

For the Use of his Scholars.

Who teaches at his School in
Queen Street near S.ᵗ Thomas Apostles.
On Mondays, Tuesdays & Wednesdays,
In the Afternoon.

ALSO

On Thursdays, Fridays & Saturdays,
In the Afternoon,
at his School next to
Furnivals Inn in Holborn.

*Ladies may be taught at
their own Houses.*

ACKNOWLEDGEMENT

I am very grateful to Clive Hurst of the Bodleian Library for
his advice on the bibliographical aspects of Kidder's book. Any
errors, of course, are entirely my own.

JJ

Text and illustrations
© Copyright the University of Oxford:
Ashmolean Museum, Oxford, 2001

Copyright in the Introduction, Bibliography, Glossary and Index of Recipe Titles,
Jane Jakeman, who has asserted her moral right to be identified as The author of
these sections

British Library Cataloguing in Publication Data
A catalogue record for this book is available from the British Library

ISBN 185444 158 2

Cover illustration: Detail from *Still-Life of Fruit and Flowers*
By Clara Peeters (*c* 1529 to about 1621)

Designed by Behram Kapadia
Printed by Clifford Press, Coventry

Contents

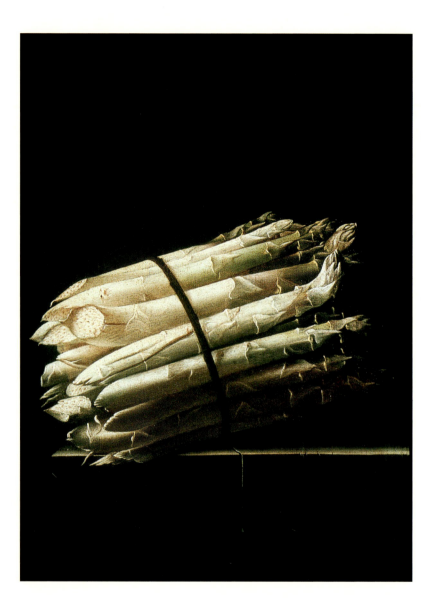

Introduction

Edward Kidder's 'Receipts' is a beautiful little book. It is historically important in rescuing for us both a fascinating collection of recipes and a particular social context. It is also an example of a form of cookery, which we may term 'Collegiate Cuisine', which is especially appropriate to Oxford.

The copy here reproduced, dating probably from the 1740s, is from the collection of Oxford University's department of the History of Art, where it is in the Hope Collection. Frederick William Hope, 1797–1862, was a graduate of Christ Church who left his wide-ranging collections, which included examples of entomology and portraiture, to the University. The book is engraved in an elegant copperplate, the work of a professional writer. At a period when printing in movable type had become the conventional method of publication, this method of book production is unusual, but gives a very attractive effect. It may have come about because Kidder was familiar with the work of the engravers who produced formal menus for banquets and grand dinners. Another possibility is that the sheets could have been sold separately, or in groups according to the subject, rather like modern 'recipe cards', in which case engraving would have looked more attractive than ordinary print.

Bibliographically, the work seems very elusive, constantly changing in its details: the Hope copy, advertising Kidder as teaching near St. Thomas Apostle's and next to Furnivall's Inn, is a version of the original edition of 1740, which was re-issued with variations on the title-page. The Bodleian, the British Library and Vassar College have further examples. There are some manuscript copies known: the University of Iowa possesses one, with the names of two owners, Sarah and Mary Prince, on the fly-leaf and a printed title-page which locates Kidder as teaching at St. Martin's le Grand and next to Furnivall's Inn. The University of Chicago has another, with a printed note locating Kidder's cookery school at 'Little Lincoln's Inn-feilds.'

Edward Kidder was probably born in Canterbury in 1667. Qualifying as a pastry cook, he moved to London where he prospered within the City.

Edward and Mary Kidder of Bedford Row had a son, also called Edward, christened in St. Andrew's, Holborn, on October 29th, 1749. It is not certain whether this was the same family as that of our pastry-master, but the surname is fairly unusual and the locations are appropriate. In the previous February, an Edward Kidder had been baptised in New Broad Street Independent Church, a non-conformist institution in the district. This baby may have been a member of a different branch of the family, but it is also possible, given that many potential patrons of his father would have been associated with the Church of England, that this is the same child. He may have been later christened in the Anglican church of St. Andrew's, and thus his family conformed to the official creed.

Edward Kidder the elder died in Holborn aged about 73. Two daughters, Elizabeth and Susan, are mentioned in his will, proved in 1739.

The various addresses reflect not only a bustling determination but indicate the nature of the work. They are all within a fairly small area of London, close to two important sources of patronage: the various Guilds of the Corporation of London, which were early trade unions of great wealth and power, and the Inns of Court, the professional bodies which trained and qualified lawyers. In the eighteenth century, both of these groups required lavish victualling and held numerous rich corporate dinners: indeed it was [and still is] a requirement of a barrister's qualification to attend dinners in an Inn of Court. For the professional cook, therefore, this area was a gold-mine, and it seems likely that Kidder was to some extent peripatetic, moving between banqueting halls as required. In the seventeen-forties, this solid bourgeois clientele was even more desirable for aspiring chefs, given the lack of opportunities at the exceeedingly dreary court of George II, whose favourite occupation was counting his money.

Although Kidder's book is attempting to address a different readership, with his offer to instruct ladies in their own homes, it is evident from the recipes that it was really a handbook for the professional cook or trainee engaged in large-scale catering. The Glossary at the end of this book contains some comments to help those who want to try contemporary versions of his recipes. Modern cooks should feel free to make some adaptations to his instructions, for some of the recipes have strong flavours for our bland modern palates, and the combinations of ingredients are sometimes surprising. The addition of anchovies to a sauce for meat, for example, is something that we would not find attractive, though this a very ancient element in European food, stretching back to the ancient Roman garum, a sauce based on salted fish. The anchovies can simply be omitted [though they would have provided a lot of salt, so the seasoning should be checked]. And the sweet dishes may need some sharpening for our tastes: a dash of lemon juice or the addition of some tart fruit would probably make Kidder's recipe for Chocolate Cream more to our liking. But looking at the book from a practical view-point, the modern domestic cook will get many ideas from Kidder, perhaps his combinations of sweet and spicy flavours or his bravura garnishes, such as finishing off a roast with oranges and lemons or cooking beef in claret tinted with cochineal. His recipes succeed in the realm of encouraging those with initiative to try something more ambitious and creative than usual, rather than as precise, scientifically-measured information for people who need instruction in every detail

When we come to placing the book in its contemporary social context, Kidder's offer, cited on his title-page, to teach women at their homes, was probably his way of trying to capture a new market through demonstrations. Hannah Glasse's cookery book, first published in 1747, which was likewise aimed at the individual household and the female market, gives recipes for many fiddly dainties, while Kidder sticks on the whole to tummy-filling pies and roasts, albeit with elaborate trimmings: one wonders what the robust lawyers and aldermen who probably formed much of Kidder's clientele would have made of Mrs. Glasse's 'pretty little sauce', or her ' number of little dishes fit for a supper.'

Hannah Glasse's first edition, advertised as 'By a Lady,' had a mainly female subscription list and was sold at 'Mrs. Ashburn's China-Shop', which was probably mostly frequented by genteel women. But it also assumed new levels of literacy: 'Every servant who can but read will be capable of making a tollerable good cook.'

This was the reasoning behind the famous cookbook of John Farley, principal chef at the London Tavern, a well-known inn.

Farley's 'London Art of Cookery and Housekeeper's Complete Assistant' described itself as 'plain and easy to the understanding of every housekeeper, cook and servant in the kingdom'.

Both Glasse and Farley included a wide range of household hints, including advice on medication and domestic chores, in order to appeal to this broad readership. Farley explicitly states that 'my intention is to instruct the lower sort', but also prefaced his work with some philosophical comments reflecting eighteenth-century views of the nature of man: 'In the early ages of the world, people lived on fruits and vegetable productions ...'.

When we turn to Kidder, we enter a different culinary kingdom, the hot and busy cockpit of the profession, less simplifying than Farley or Glasse, more exciting, too busy to indulge in moralising. Knowledge of the basic processes, of the elementary skills of choosing meat or timings, is assumed. What Kidder offers is the preparation of more elaborate and dramatic creations, food that can be dished up with a flourish, with large-scale planning for many diners.

The frontispiece depicting Kidder, and showing a lively, somewhat choleric, countenance, is by Robert Shepherd, a well-known engraver. The portrait was probably the reason for the book's inclusion in Hope's collection, but the work is very appropriate in a University collection, for the cuisine suitable for the corporate dinners of aldermen and lawyers was also eminently adaptable to the colleges of the University. It is not just a matter of scale, but that these institutions acted as all-male dining clubs, conservative in their tastes, demanding a heavy supply of pastries and puddings, with some elaborate dishes that could be carried in to the sound of applause on feast days, such as the recipes for swan pie and boar's head [the latter being the centrepiece of the famous Christmas feast at The Queen's

College]. The flirtatious sexual atmosphere implied by recipes in earlier books intended for aristocratic households, such as the seventeenth century cookery book of Robert May, which featured an imitation pie with live frogs, which would make 'the ladies to skip and shriek', would be inappropriate at such gatherings.

The Hope copy of Kidder's work is not just a library specimen but has been tried and tested in the past. 'Good', written alongside the recipe for Carrot Pudding may well be the comment of some eighteenth-century college cook.

Indeed, there are many similarities between Kidder's recipes and those of Ralph Ayres, an eighteenth-century New College chef whose manuscript recipe book is now in the Bodleian Library [Ms. Don.e.89]. They both have almost the same elaborate instructions for Calf's Head Hash, for example, adding oysters, mushrooms, anchovies and fried forcemeat balls to the dish. Kidder supplies a recipe for the 'Veal Olives' which Ayres specifies as additions to the calf's head; both have comparable recipes for 'Wiggs', little cakes served in Lent, and for 'Quaking Pudding', and similar traditional confections.

The two-course arrangement set out in Kidder's 'Order for Bills of Fare' is standard for large entertainments at this period and is reflected in accounts of College dinners. [I think Kidder is merely indicating which dishes are appropriate for each course, not that everything listed should appear on the table.] Graham Midgley, in 'University Life in Eighteenth-century Oxford', quotes a dinner at Christchurch where the first course included cod, mutton, soup, chicken pie, puddings, and vegetables, and the second pigeons, asparagus, veal, sweetbreads, lobster, apricot tart, syllabubs and jellies. Sweet items were served as part of the second course, at the same time as mixed savoury dishes. Fruit and dessert wines were usually served afterwards.

These lavish dinners were appreciated by the dons but some of Kidder's recipes would have been welcome in other quarters in the University. He was evidently especially noted as a pastry-master, and includes instructions for a splendid variety of pies and fillings, along with templates for pastry cutters to provide appropriate trimmings. [Pies were not only raised or flat containers for mixed fillings, but pastry cases for birds and joints of meat.]

Hungry undergraduates have always been particularly fond of traditional stodge in the form of pasties and pies. Here again, Kidder's culinary style would have been much appreciated in Oxford, where his little book still finds a good home.

JANE JAKEMAN

All Sorts of Paste

Kidders Receipts.

1

All sorts of Paste

Puff Paste.

Lay down a pound of flower; break into it 2 ounces of butter & 2 eggs; then make it into Paste with cold water; then work the other part of the pound of butter to the stiffness of your paste; then roul out yo'. paste into a Square Sheet: Stick it all over with bitts of butter; flower it, and roul it up like a collar, double it up at both ends that they meet in y' middle, roul it out again as aforesaid, till all the pound of butter is in.

Paste for a Pasty.

Lay down a Peck of flower, work it up with six pound of butter and four eggs with cold water.

Paste for a high Pye.

Lay down a peck of flower and work it up with 3 pound of butter melted in a Sauce-pan of boyling liquor and make it into a stiff paste

Paste Royal :

for Patty Pans.

Lay down a pound of flower and work it up with ½ a pound of butter, 2 ounces of fine Sugar & 4 eggs.

Paste for a Custard.

Lay down flower and make it into a stiff Paste with boyling water; sprinkle it with cold water, to keep it from cracking.

A

Kidders Receipts. 2

Forc'd Meat Balls.

Sweet Balls.

Take part of a Leg of Lamb or Veal & Scrape it fine & shred the same quantity of Beef Suet; put thereto a good quantity of Currants, Season it with Sweet Spice, a little Lemon Peel, 3 or 4 Yolks of eggs, & a few Sweet-herbs; mix it well together & make it into little balls

Savoury Balls

Take part of a Leg of Lamb or Veal & Scrape it fine with the same quantity minc'd of beef Suet, a little lean bacon, Sweet-herbs, a Shallot & Anchovie, beat it in a Mortar till it is as Smooth as wax, Season it with Savoury Spice & make it into little balls.

Another way

Take the flesh of Fowl, Beef Suet & Marrow the same quantity 6 or 8 Oysters, lean-bacon, Sweet-herbs, & Savoury Spice, pound it & make it into little balls.

Fish Balls

Take Carp & Eel, mince with it the same quantity of Suet, Sweet-herbs & Savoury Spice, bread & eggs; beat it in a mortar & make it into Balls.

A Caudle for Sweet Pyes

Take Sack & white-wine alike in quantity a little Verjuice & Sugar; boyl it & brew it, with 2 or 3 Eggs as butter'd Ale, when the Pyes are bak'd, pour it in at the Funnel & shake it togather.

A.1.

Kidder's Receipts. 3

A Lear for Savoury Pyes.

Take Claret gravy Oyster liquor, 2 or 3 Anchovies, a faggot of Sweet-herbs & an Onion boyl it up & thicken it with brown butter; then pour it in to your Savoury Pyes when call'd for.

A Lear for Fish Pyes.

Take Claret white Wine, Vineager, Oyster-Liquor, Anchovies & drawn butter; when ye Pyes are bak'd, pour it in with the Funnel.

A Lear for Pasties.

Season the bones of that meat you make your Pasty off, cover them with water & bake them with the Pasty when bak'd, strain the liquor out into the Pasty.

A Ragoo for Made Dishes.

Take Claret gravy, Sweet-herbs and Savoury Spice toss up in it Lamb-stones, Cox-Combes, boil'd, blanch'd & slic'd with slic'd Sweet-breads, Oysters, Mushrooms, Truffells & Murrells, thicken these with brown butter; use it when call'd for.

A Regalia of Cowcumbers.

Take Twelve Cowcumbers and Slice them as for eating, beat and Squeeze them very dry; flower and fry them brown, then put to them Claret, gravy, Savoury Spice and a bit of butter rouled up in flower; toss them up thick, they are Sauce for Mutton or Lamb.

A.2.

Sweet Pyes

Kidders Receipts.   4

Sweet Pyes
A Lamb Pye

Cut a hind quarter of Lamb into thin Slices season it with Sweet Spice & lay it in the Pye mixt with half a pound of raisons of the Sun Ston'd, ½ a pound of Currants, 2 or 3 Spainish Pottatoes, boil'd, blanch'd & Slic'd or an Artichoke bottom or two, with Prunellas Damsons Goosberries, Grapes, Citron & Lemon Chips, lay on butter & close the Pye; when 'tis bak'd make for it a Caudle.

A Chicken Pye

Take 6 Small Chickens roul up a piece of butter in Sweet Spice & put it into them, then season them & lay them in the Pye with ÿ marrow of 2 bones with fruit & preserves as the Lamb Pye with a Caudle.

Minc'd Pyes.

Shred a pound of neats tongue parboil'd wth two pound of beef Suet 5 Pippins & a green Lemon Peel: Season it with an Ounce of Sweet Spice, a pound of Sugar; 2 pound of Currants, ½ a pint of Sack, a little Orange flower water, the juyce of 3 Lemons, a quarter of a pound of Citron Lemon and Orange peel: mix these togather & fill your pyes

Sweet Spice is Cloves, Mace, Nutmeg, Cinnamon, Sugar & Salt.

B

Kidder's Receipts.

Egg Pyes.

Shred the Yolks of 20 hard eggs w.th Citron and Lemon peel, Season it with Sweet Spice, then mix them with a quart of custard Stuff ready made, gather it to a body over the fire, your pies being dry'd in the Oven, fill them with this batter as Custards, when bak'd Stick them with Slic'd citron, and Strew them with coloured biskets.

Another way.

Shred the yolks of 20 eggs with the Same weight of marrow and beef Suet, Season it with sweet Spice with Citron and Lemon, fill and close the pyes.

A Lumber Pye.

Take a pound and a half of a fillet of Veal & mince it with the Same quantity of beef Suet, Season it with Sweet Spice, 5 pippins an handfull of Spinnage and an hard lettice, thyme and parsley, mix it with a penny grated white loaf; the yolks of 2 or 3 eggs, Sack and Orange flower water, a pound & an ½ of Currants & preserves as the lamb pye & a caudle. An Humble Pye is made the Same way.

An Artichoke Pye.

Take the bottoms of 6 or 8 artichokes being boil'd & slic'd, Season them with Sweet Spice, and mix them with the marrow of 3 bones, with fruit & preserves as y^e lamb pye and a caudle. A Skerret or Pottatoe Pye's made the Same way.

B.1.

Savoury Pyes
Sweet Spice

Kidders Receipts.

5

Savoury Pyes.
A Lamb Pye.

Cut an hind quarter of Lamb into thin Slices, Season it with Savoury Spice and lay them in the Pye with an hard Lettice & Artichoke bottoms, the top of an hundred of Asparragus, lay on butter and close y̆ Pye; when it is bak'd pour into it a Lear

A Mutton Pye.

Season your mutton stakes with savoury Spice, fill the Pye, lay on butter and close the Pye; when it is bak'd, toss up an handfull of chopt capers, Cowcumbers & Oysters in gravy, an anchovy & drawn butter.

A Hare Pye.

Cut it in pieces, Season & lay it in the pye with balls, Slic'd lemon butter and close the pye.

A Hen Pye.

Cut it in pieces, Season it and lay it in the Pye with balls, yolks of hard eggs, Slic'd lemon butter & close the pye: when it is bak'd, pour in a Lear thicken'd with eggs.

A Pidgeon Pye.

Truss and season your Pidgeons wth Savoury Spice, lard them wth bacon & stuff y̆. wth forc'd meat & lay y̆. in y̆ pye wth ingredients for Savoury pyes wth butter & close y̆ pye a Lear: A Chicken or Capon pye's made y̆ same way.

C

Kidders Receipts.

A Battalia Pye.

Take 4 Small Chickens, 4 Squob Pidgeons, 4 Sucking Rabbits, cut them in pieces, Season it with Savoury Spice and lay them in the pye with 4 Sweetbreads Sliced and as many Sheeps tongues, 2 Shiver'd pallats, 2 pair of Lamb Stones, 20 or 30 cocks combs with Savoury balls & Oysters, lay on butter & close the pye A Lear.

A Calves head Pye.

Almost boyl the Calves head, take out all the bones and cut it into thin Slices and lay it in the pye with the Ingredients for Savoury pyes. A Lear.

A Neats Tongue Pye

Half boyl the Tongues blanch & Slice them Season them with Savoury Spice, wth balls slic'd Lemon and butter; and close the Pye: when it is bak'd pour into it a Ragooe.

A Venison Pye.

Raise a round high pye, then shred a pound of beef Suet and put it in the bottom, cut your Venison in pieces and Season it with pepper and Salt and lay it on the Suet, lay on butter and close ye pye and bake it Six hours.

Sweet Spice is Cloves Mace, Nutmeg, Cinnamon and Salt; if for meat pyes, Fowls or Fish with a little fine pepper: Savoury Spice is Pepper, Salt, Cloves, Mace & Nutmeg.

C.1.

Kidders Receipts.

Cold Pyes.

A Veal Pye

Raise an high pye, then cut a Fillet of Veal into 3 or 4 Fillets, Season it with Savoury Spice, a little minc'd Sage and Sweetherbs, lay it in ye Pye with Slices of bacon at the bottom & betwixt each piece, lay on butter and close the pye.

A Swan Pye

Skin and bone your Swan. Lard it with bacon and Season it with Savoury Spice & a few bay Leaves powder'd, lay it in the pye, Stick it with cloves, lay on butter and close the pye.

A Turkey Pye.

Bone the Turkey, Season it with savoury Spice and lay it in the pye with 2 Capons or 2 wild ducks cut in pieces to fill up the corners, lay on butter and close the pye.

A Goose Pye

Is made the Same way with 2 Rabbits.

All cold Pyes,

when they are bak'd and half cold must be filled up with Clarrify'd butter.

To make Catchup.

Take a pt. of Clarret a pt. of Vineager & 6 ounces of Anchovys & whole Spice, boyle it together till it's dissolv'd Strain it thro a fine Sive and keep it in a bottle.

C.2.

Kidders Receipts. 7

Fish Pyes.
A Carp Pye.

Bleed your carp at the tail, open the belly draw &
wash out the blood w.th a little clarret, vineager & Salt,
then season your carp with savoury Spice & shread sweet
herbs, lay it in the pye with a pint of large oysters, butter and close the pye when it is bak'd put into the lear; y.
blood & clarret and pour it into the pye.

A Trout Pye.

Cut wash and Scale them lard them with pieces
of a Silver eel rould up in Spice and Sweetherbs and
bay leaves powder'd lay on and between them Sliced
Artichoke bottoms, mushrooms, oysters, capers dic'd lemon, lay on butter and close the pye.

An Eel Pye.

Cut and Season them with Spice, an handfull of
currants, butter and close the pye.
A Lamprey Pye is made the Same way
with dic'd lemon and citron.

An Oyster Pye.

Parboyl a quart of large Oysters in their
own liquor, mince them Small and pound them in a
mortar with pistachonuts, marrow and Sweet-herbs,
an onion and Savoury Spice and a little grated bread
or Season them as aforesaid whole, lay on butter
and close the pye.

C.3.

Florendines & Puddings

Kidders Receipts. 8

Florendines & Puddings.

A Florendine of a Kidney of Veal.

Shread the kidney fat & all with a little Spinnage, parsley and lettice, 3 pippins and orange peel; Season it with Sweet Spice and Sugar and a good handfull of currants; 2 or 3 grated biskets Sack & Orange flower water, 2 or 3 eggs, mix it into a body and put it in a dish being covered w.th puff past lay on a cut-lid and garnish the brim.

A Florendine of oranges & apples

Cut 6 Sevil oranges in halves, save the juice pull out the pulp and lay them in water 24 hours shifting them 3 or 4 times then boyl them in 3 or 4 waters; in the 4.th water put to them a pound of fine Sugar and their juyce; boyl them to a Syrrup, & keep them in this Syrrup in an earthen pot; when you use y.m cut them in thin Slices Two of these Oranges will make a Florendine, mixt with 10 pippins pared, quartered & boyl'd up in water and Sugar; lay them in a dish being cover'd & garnish'd as before

A Rice Florendine

Boyl ½ a pound of rice tender in fair water, y.n put to it a quart of milk or cream boyl it thick & season it with Sweet Spice & Sugar mix it w.th 8 eggs well beat ½ a pound of currants ½ a pound of butter & y.e marrow of two bones, 3 grated biskets, Sack and orange flower water, put it in a dish being cover ed & garnish'd as aforesaid.

D.

Kidders Receipts.

A Tort de moy

Blanch ½ a pound of jordan almonds & beat them in a mortar with a quarter of a p.nd of citron, y^e white of a capon, 4 grated Biskets sweet Spice and sugar, Sack and orange flower water: then mix it with a pint of cream and 7 eggs being well beat and the marrow of 2 bones in pieces; then bring all these ingredients to a body over ye fire & put it in a dish being cover'd and garnished with puff paste.

A Marrow Pudding.

Boyl a quart of cream or milk with a stick of cinnamon a quarter'd nutmeg and large mace, then mix it with 8 eggs well beat; a little Salt, Sugar, Sack and orange flower water, strain it, then put to it, 3 grated biskets, an handfull of currants, as many raysons of the Sun, the marrow of 2 bones all to 4 large pieces: then gather it to a body over ye fire & put it in a dish having the brim thereof garnished with puff past and rais'd in the oven: then lay on the 4 pieces of marrow, colour'd knots & pasts, slic'd citron and lemon peel.

An Almond Pudding.

Take ½ a pound of jordan almonds, blanch & pound y^m. in a mortar wth. 4 grated biskets and three quarters of a pound of butter, Sack & orang flower water, then mix it wth a quart of cream being boyl'd & mixt wth 8 eggs sweet spice & Sugar, pour it into y^e. dish being cover'd & garnish'd wth puff paste.

D.1.

Kidders Receipts.

A Carrot Pudding.

Boyl 2 large carrots, when cold pound them, in a mortar, Strain them thro a Sive, mix them wth two grated biskets, ½ a pound of butter, Sack and Orange flower water, Sugar and a little Salt, a pint of cream mixt with 7 yolks of eggs and two whites, beat these together and put them in a dish covered and garnished. Good

A Calves foot Pudding.

Take 2 calves feet shred them very fine, mix them with a penny loaf grated & scalded wth a pint of cream put to it ½ a p^nd of shred beef suet & eggs & a hand full of plumpt currants, Season it wth sweet spice & sugar a little sack & orange flower water, ye marrow of 2 bones y^n put it in a veal caul being wash'd over wth ye batter of eggs, then wet a cloth & put it therein, tye it close up, w^n ye pot boyls put it in, boyl it about 2 hours, y^n turn it in a dish, Stick on it slic'd almonds & citron, let the sauce be, Sack & orange flower water wth lemon juyce Sugar & drawn butter.

An Orange Pudding.

Take ye peels of 2 Sevil Oranges boyl'd up as for a florendine of oranges & apples, pound & season y^m as ye Carrots.

A quaking Pudding.

Take a q^rt of cream & beat 3 or 4 spoonfulls wth 3 or 4 spoonfulls of flower of rice, a penny loaf grated & 7 eggs orange flower water sugar & sweet spice, butter the cloth & tye it up but not too close, boyl it about an hour Stick on it slic'd citron, let ye sauce be Sack & orange flower water lemon juyce Sugar & drawn butter.

D.2.

Kidders Receipts.

A Tansey

Boyl a quart of cream or milk w.th a stick of cinnamon, quarter'd nutmeg, and large mace; when half cold mix it with 20 yolks of eggs and 10 whites strain it, then put to it 4 grated biskets, ½ a pound of butter, a pint of Spinnage juice, and a little Tansey Sack and orange flower water; Sugar & a little Salt; then gather it to a body over the fire and pour it into your dish being well butter'd when it is bak'd turn it on a pye plate; Squeese on it an orange grate on Sugar and garnish it with Slic'd orange and a little tansey made in a plate cut as you please, good

A Custard

Boyl a quart of cream or milk, with a Stick of Cinnamon quarter'd Nutmeg and large Mace when half cold, mix it with eight yolks of eggs & four whites well beat Sugar Sack and Orange flower water. Set it on the fire and Stirr it untill a white froth ariseth, Schum it off then fill your custard being dry'd in the Oven. good

An Almond Custard.

Blanch and pound them in a mortar very fine: in the beating add thereto a little milk press it through a Sive, and make it as your aforesaid custard. A Torte of Artechokes or Winsor beans boyle blanch & pound y.m w.th almonds citron lemon & orange piele & 2 biskits mixt w.th custard stuff & gather'd

D.3.

Cakes

Kidders Receipts.

9

Cakes.

A Plumb Cake

Take 6 pound of Currants, 5 Pound of Flower an ounce of Cloves & Mace, a little Cinnamon ½ an Ounce of Nutmeg; ½ a P.ⁿᵈ of pounded & blanch'd Almonds; ½ a P.ᵈ of Sugar, 3 quart.ʳˢ of a pound of Slic'd Citron, Lemon & Orange Peel; ½ a pint of Sack, a little honey water & a quart of ale yest; a quart of Cream, 2 Pound and ½ of butter melted & pour'd into the middle thereof; then Strew a little flower thereon & let it lye to rise, then work it well together, then lay it before ⅄ fire to rise ⁿ work it up till it is very Smooth, then put it in an hoop with a paper flower'd at the bottom.

The Iceing.

Beat & Sift a pound & an half of double refin'd Sugar & put to it the whites of 6 eggs, put in but one at a time & beat them in a bason w.ᵗʰ a silver spoon till it be very light and white.

A Seed Cake

Take 2 pound of Smooth Carraways, 6 pound of flower; ½ a pound of Sugar, an ounce of Sweet Spice with Citron, Lemon peele; then make an hole in ⅄ flower & put in ½ a pint of yest & 8 eggs well beat, ½ a pint of Sack, a little Orange flower water; a pint of Cream & 2 pound of butter warm'd together, then strew a little flower thereon, let it lye to rise then put it in an hoop and strew over it double refin'd Sugar and rough Carraways.

E.

Kidders Receipts.

A Light Seed Cake

Take ½ a quartern of flower a little ginger, Nutmeg, 3 Spoonfulls of ale yest & 3 eggs well beat, 3 quarters of a pint of milk, ½ a pound of butter and 6 Ounces of Smooth carraways, work it warm together with your hand

Portugal Cakes.

Put a pound of fine Sugar, a pound of fresh butter, 5 eggs & a little beaten mace into a flat pan beat it up with your hands till it is very light, y.ⁿ put thereto a pound of flower, ½ a pound of currants very clean pickt and dry'd; beat them together, fill your heart pans and bake them in a Slack Oven

You may make Seed Cakes the Same way: only put carraway Seeds instead of currants.

Shrewsbury Cakes.

Take a pound of fresh butter, a pound of double refin'd Sugar sifted, a little beaten mace and 4 eggs, beat them all together with your hands till it is very light: then put thereto a pound and ½ of flower and roul them out into little Cakes.

Ginger-bread Cakes.

Take 3 pound of flower, a pound of Sugar and a pound of butter rubb'd very fine, an Ounce of ginger and a grated nutmeg; mix it with a pound and a quarter of treacle: then make it up stiff, roul it out & cut them in little Cakes and bake them in a Slack Oven

E.1.

Kidders Receipts.

Another way.

Take a quartern of flower, 2 pound and 3 quarters of treacle and ½ a pound of butter warm'd together,
an Ounce of Ginger, ½ an Ounce of Carraway and Cori-
ander Seeds bruis'd make it into large Cakes put into ei-
ther of them what Sweet meats you please when they
are bak'd dip them in boiling water to glaze them

Cheese Cakes.

Take the curd of a gallon of milk, 3 quarters of
a pound of fresh butter, 2 grated biskets, 2 Ounces of
blanch'd Almonds pounded with a little Sack and
Orange flower water, ½ a pound of Currants and 7 Eggs
Spice and Sugar, beat it up with a little Cream till it is
very light; then fill your Cheese-cakes

Ingredients for sweet Pyes.

The meat Fish or Fowls.

Spice balls, Citron Lemon and Orange Peel; Spanish
Potatoes, Skerrets, Reasons, Currants, Grapes, Goosberrys
and Damsons, a Caudle.

For Savoury Pyes.

The meat Fish or Fowls.

Savoury Spice, balls, bacon, Shiver'd Pallats
Lamb Stones, Coxcombs and Stones, Hearty-Choke
bottoms, Oysters, Mushroons, Truffle & Morells.

Wiggs Take a quartern of flower, ½ a p.^{d} of Sugar
an handfull of Carraway seed: then put into y^e middle of the
flower ½ a p.^{nt} of yest wth a p.nd & ½ of butter melted in a p^t
of milk & pour'd to y^e yest stirring it wth yor hands stren flower
let them lye to rise, then E.2 make up yor wiggs.

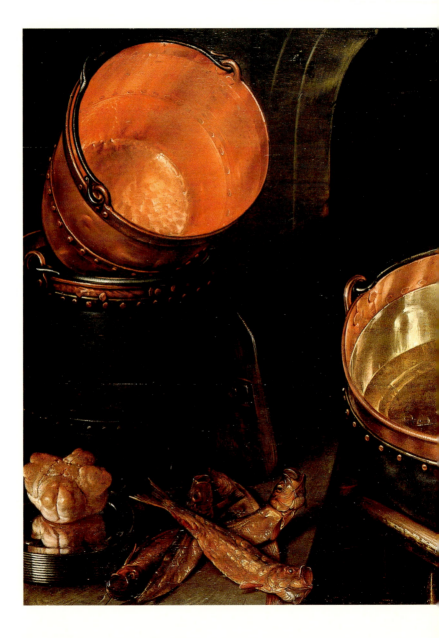

Broths and Pottages

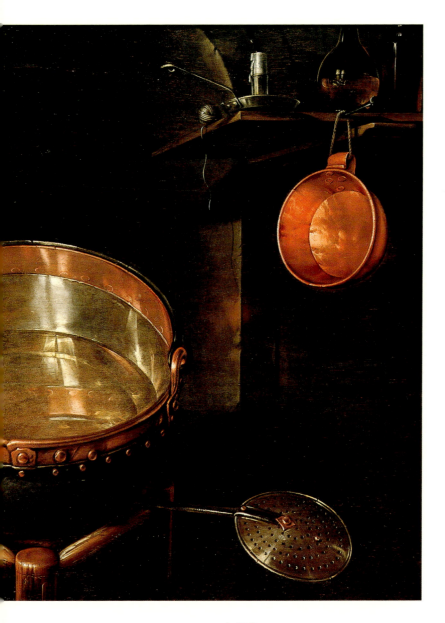

Kidders Receipts.

10

Broths and Pottages.

Strong-broth.

Take 3 or 4 gallons of water and put therein a leg
and shinn of beef, and a crag of mutton cut into pieces,
boyle it 12 hours, now and then stir it with a stick and
cover it close: when it is boyl'd strain and cool it, let it
stand till 'twill jelly, then take the fatt from the top &
the dreß from the bottom

Gravey.

Cut a piece of beef into thinn slices and fry it
brown in a stew-pan with 2 or 3 onions, 2 or 3 lean
slices of bacon then pour to it a ladle or 2 of Strong
broth, rubbing the brown off from the pan very clean
add to it more Strong broth, clarret, white wine anchovies, a faggot of Sweetherbs, Seafon it and let it
Stew very well, then Strain it off.

Brown Pottage Royall.

Set gallon of Strong broth on the fire with 2 Shiver'd
pallats, coxcombs, lambstones slic'd with Savoury-
balls, a pint of gravy, 2 handfulls of Spinnage & young
lettice minc'd boyl thefe together with a duck the leg &
wing bones being broke and pull'd out and the breast
Slash'd and brown'd in a pan of fatt then put to it 2
french rowls slic'd and dry'd hard and brown. Then
put the Pottage in a dish and duck in the middle, lay a
bout it a little vermachelly boyl'd up in a little Strong broth
with Savoury balls and Sweetbreads garnish it with
Scalded parsley turnips, beat root and barberries.

F.

Kidders Receipts.

A White Soop.

Boyl ½ a pound of rice tender in water & milk then put to it 2 quarts of Strong broth, herbs, balls, a french rowl cut in dice and all fry'd Season it, and put a forc'd chicken in the middle.

A Crawfish Soop

Cleanse your crawfish and boyl them in wat.^r Salt and Spice, pull off their feet and tails and fry y.^m break the rest of them in a Stone mortar; Season them with Savoury Spice and an onion, hard eggs, grated bread and Sweetherbs boyl'd in Strong broth; strain it; then put to it Scalded chopt parsley & french rowls, then put them therein with a few dry'd mushrooms; garnish the dish with slic'd lemon and the feet and tails of the crawfish. A Lobster Soop is done the same way.

Peas Soop.

Boyl a quart of good Seed peas tender & thick, Strain and wash it thrô with a pint of milk: then put thereto a quart of Strong broth boyl'd with balls, a little Spire mint and a dry'd French rowl and Season it with pepper and Salt

Plum-pottage

Take two gallons of Strong broth; put to it two pound of currants, two pound of raisons of the Sun, half an ounce of sweet Spice, a pound of Sugar a quart of clarret, a pint of Sack, the juice of three oranges and three lemons; thicken it with grated biskets, or rice flower with a pound of pruants.

F.1.

Kidder^s Receipts.

To boyl Pullets & Oysters.

Boyl them in water and Salt, with a good piece of bacon: for Sauce draw up a pound of butter with a little white-wine, Strong broth and a quart of oysters: then put your 3 pullets in a dish cut your bacon and lay it about them, nth a pound and ½ of fry'd Sauceages and garnish it with Sliced lemon. Or you may boyl your pullets in bladders and Send them up in a ragove.

To Boyl Rabbits.

Truss them for boyling and lard them nth bacon; then boyl them quick and white: for ye sauce take the boyl'd liver Shread it with fat bacon, tofs these up together in Strong broth, white wine & vineager, mace, Salt and nutmeg minc'd, Selt parsley, Barberries & drawn butter then lay your Rabbits in a dish; pour ye lear all over them and garnish it with Slic'd lemon and barberries

To Boyl Pidgeons.

Stuff your Pidgeons with Sweet-herbs, chopt, bacon, a little grated bread, butter and Spice, the yolk of an egg: tye them at both ends and boyl them as aforesaid, and garnish them with slic'd lemon & barberries.
Forcd Chickens, lay in y^e bottom of the pan slices of bacon & beef, savory spice & sweet herbs, lay in y^e Chickens y^n lay on y^e slic'dbeef, bacon & cover y^e close wth F. . past or cover & a ragove.

Kidders Receipts. 11

Made Dishes.

Scotcht Collops.

Take the skin from a Fillet of Veal & cut it into thin Collops, hack and Scotch them with ye back
of a knife, lard half of them with bacon & fry them
with a little brown butter, then take them out & put them
into another tossing pan, then set the pan they were
fry'd in over the fire again, wash it out wth a little
strong broth rubbing it with your ladle, then pour it
to the Collops, do this to every pansull till all are
fry'd; then Stew & toss them up with a pint of Oysters,
2 Anchovies, 2 Shiver'd pallats, cocks combs, lambstones,
& Sweetbreads blanch'd & Sliced, savory balls, onions,
a faggot of Sweetherbs; thicken it with brown butter & garnish it with Slic'd Orange.

Olives of Veal.

Take 8 or 10 Scotcht Collops wash them over wth
the batter of eggs, then Season & lay over them a little
forc'd meat, roul them up & roast them, then make for
them a ragooe, & garnish it with Slic'd Orange.

Chickens forc'd wth Oysters.

Lard & Truss them, make a forcing of oysters,
Sweetherbs, Parsley, Truffells, Mushrooms, & Onions; chop these together and Season it, mix it with a
piece of butter the yolk of an egg then tye them at both
ends and roast them; then make for them a Ragooe &
garnish them with Slic'd Lemon.

F 3.

Kidders Receipts.

Bombarded Veal.

Take a fillet of veal cut out of it 5 lean pieces, as thick as your hand, round them up a little, then lard them very thick on the round side, lard 5 sheeps tongues being boyl'd blanch'd & larded wth lemon peel & beet root, y^n make a well seasoned forc'd meat, wth Veal, lean Bacon beef Suet & an anchovy, roul it up into a ball being well beat y^n make another tender forc'd meat with veal, fat bacon, beef Suet, mushrooms, Spinnage, parsley, thyme, Sweet marjoram, winter Savoury and green onions Season and beat it. Then put your forc'd ball into part of this forc'd meat, put it in a veal caul & bake it in a little pot; then roul up that which is left in another veal caul, wet with the batter of eggs, roul it up like a polonia Sauceage, tye it at both ends & Slightly round and boyl it. Your forc'd ball being bak'd, put it in the middle of the dish, yor Larded Veal being stew'd in strong broth lay round it & ye tongues fry'd brown between each, then pour on them a ragooe, lay about it the other forc'd meat cut as thinn as a half Crown and fry'd in the batter of eggs then squeese on it an Orange and garnish it with slic'd Lemon

Pigeons in Comport.

Truss Lard & Force your pidgeon's being Seasoned Stew them in Strong broth and make for them a ragooe and garnish them with sweetbreads, Sippits and Sprigs of parsley, all fry'd in the batter of eggs, and Slic'd Lemon Thus you may garnish most made dishes.

F.4.

Kidders Receipts.

A Calves-head hash'd.

YOUR Calves head being slitt & cleans'd, half boyl'd & cold: cut One Side into thin Slices and fry it in butter, then having a tossing pan on the Stow with a Ragooe for made dishes, toss it up and stew it together: then Scotch the other Side cross and cross, flower, bast and broyle it. The hash being thicken'd with brown butter, put it in the dish, lay ov.^r & about it fry'd balls and the tongue Slic'd and larded with bacon, lemon peel and beat root; then fry in the batter of eggs, Slic'd Sweetbreads, carv'd Sippets and Oysters, lay in the head, and place these on & about the dish and garnish it with Slic'd Orange and Lemon.

A Ragooe of a breast of veal.

BONE a breast of veal, cut a handsom Square piece; then cut the other part into Small pieces, brown it in butter, then stew and toss it up in your ragooe for made dishes, thicken it with brown butter; then put the ragooe in ye dish lay on the Square piece, dic'd lemon, Sweetbreads, Sippets, and bacon fry'd in the batter of eggs, and garnish it with Slic'd Orange.

A Ragooe of Sweet breads.

SET, Lard and Force the Sweet-breads w.th mushrooms, the tender ends of pallats, cocks combs, boyl'd tender, beat it in a mortar mixt w.th fine herbs; and Spice, a little grated bread and an egge or two; then fry them thus forc'd, and toss them up in a ragooe, thicken it with brown butter, & Squeese in it a lemon, garnish it with Slic'd lemon & barberries.

F. 5.

Kidders Receipts.

Beeff Alamode.

Take a good buttock of beef, interlarded w:th great lard rould up in savoury Spice & Sweet-herbs; put it in a great Sauce pan & cover it close & Sett it in y^e oven all night, this is fit to eat cold.

Veal Alamode Ala Daub.

Take a good fillet of veal interlarded as ye beef, ad to ye stewing of it a little white wine; then make for it a ragooe & garnish it with slic'd lemon.

A Pompetone of Pidgeons or Larks.

Take your savoury forc'd meat & roul it out as past, & put it in a tossing pan, then lay in thin slices of bacon, Squob pidgeons, slic'd sweetbreads, tops of asparagus, mushrooms, yolks of hard eggs, ye tender ends of shiver'd pallats & cocks combs boyl'd, blanch'd & slic'd: then cover it over with another forc'd meat as a pye when bak'd, turn it in a dish & pour into it a gravy.

Pidgeon Pears.

Bone your pidgeons all but one leg, and put ye thro. ye side out at ye vent; cut of ye toes & fill them w:th forc'd meat, made of ye heart & liver, & cover them with a tender forc'd meat being wash'd with ye batter of eggs; & shape them like pears; yⁿ. wash y^m. over & roul y^m. in scalded chopt spinnage, cover y^m. wth thin Slices of bacon, & put y^m. in bladders, boyl y^m. an hour & ½, then take them out of the bladders and lay y^m. before the fire to crisp them, then make for y^m a raggooe.

F 6

Kidders Receipts.

A Goose Turkey or Leg of Mutton, a la Daub.

Lard it with bacon and half roast it, draw it of
the spit and put it in as small a pot as will boyl it
put to it a quart of white wine strong broth a pint
of vineager, whole spice, bay leaves, sweet marjoram
winter savoury & green onions: when tis ready lay it
in ye dish: make sauce wth. some of y liquor, mushrooms dic'd
lemon: 2 or 3 anchovies: thicken it with brown butter &
garnish it with slic'd lemon.

Oyster Loaves.

Cut a round hole in the tops of 5 french rouls and
take out all y crumb, & smear y^m over y^e sides wth a tender forc'd meat of sett oysters & part of an eele: y^n fry y^m
crisp in lard & fill $y^m w^{th}$ a quart of oysters: y^e rest of y
eel cut like lard, spice, mushrooms anchovys toss'd up in y liq.
& $\frac{1}{2}$ a pint of white-wine; thicken it with a bit of butter rould up in flower.

Sauceages.

Take pork more lean than fat & shred it, then
take of y flake of pork & mince it: season each a part w^{th}.
minc'd sage, & pretty high w. savoury spice: y^n clear y^e.
small gutts & fill y^m mixing some bitts of fat & a little wine wth it; then tye them in links.

Polonia Sauceages.

Take a peice of red gammon of bacon and half boyl it
mince it wth as much bacon lard, minc'd sage, thyme & savoury
spice, y^e yolks of eggs & as much red wine as will bring it to a pretty thick body; mix $y^m w^{th}$ yor hands & fill y^m in large skins &
dry them as hamms.

F 7

Kidder's Receipts.

To Boil a Haunch of Venison.

Your venison being Salted 2 or 3 days stuff
it in holes with beef Suet, Sweet herbs & Spice,
hard eggs grated bread & a raw egg: when
boyl'd lay it in the dish with Colliflowers or
Cabbage Carrots or Turnips

To roast a haunch of Venison

Spit & cover it w.th thick paper & roast it basting
it w.th a q.^{t} of water & $\frac{1}{2}$ a p.^{d} of salt in y^e pan till its
all dry, then pull off y^e paper & drudg it w.th grated
bread & flower & bast it w.th almost a p.^{d} of butter
when its roasted lay it in y^e dish with gravy & Set
your Gallendine in China basons

You may make Olives or Scotcht Collops of a
haunch of Venison, as of Veal.

Gallendine or Venison Sauce.

Boyl clarret grated bread whole Cinnamon Ginger
mace a Sprig of rosemary vineager & Sugar boild up y.^{ch}

To Roast a Fillet of Beef.

Take out ye fillet of ye inside of a Sir Loyne of beef,
and lard it with bacon like a hare & lay in a pan &
pour on it a marronnade of vineager lemon juice
crackt pepper broken mace slic'd nutmeg ginger an on
ion & sweet herbs let it lye 2 h.^{rs} y^n spit it between 8 squers bast
& drudge it w.th bread & flower & make for it a ragove.
Thus you marronnade any fowls sweetbreads or collops.

F 8

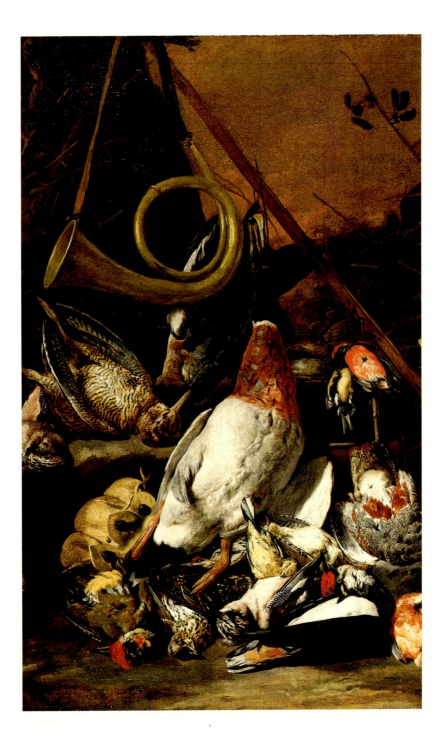

Kidders Receipts.

To roast an Hare

Sett and lard it with bacon make for it a pudding of grated bread the heart and liver being parboiled and chopt small with beef Suet and sweetherbs mix with marrow cream spice & eggs then sew up the belly and roast him when 'tis roasted let yo.r butter be drawn up with cream gravy or clarret.

To roast it with the Skin on

Make the pudding as aforsaid Sew up y belly & thrust yo.r hand round him between the Skin and his body, and rub over his flesh with butter & Spice, & sew up the hole of the Skin & roast him basting of him with boyling water & Salt till it is above half roasted, then let him dry & the Skin smoke, pull it of by piec's then bast him with butter; drudg him with flower, bread & Spice, Sauce him as aforesaid & ganish it n.th slic'd bacon.

A Leg of Mutton a la Royal

Lard your mutton and Slices of veal n.th bacon rouled in Spice and Sweet-herbs then bringing them to a brown in melted lard, boylthe leg of mutton in Strong broth, all Sorts of Sweet-herbs, an onion Stuck n.th cloves when it is ready lay it in the dish lay round it the Collops y n pour on it a Ragooe and garnish it n.th lemon & oranges.

G

Kidders Receipts.

A brown Fricasse of Chickens or Rabbits.

Cut them in pieces & fry them in butter. then, having ready hot a pint of gravy, a little Clarret whitewine & Strong broth, 2 anchovys, 2 Shiver'd pallats, a faggot of Sweet-herbs, Savoury balls & Spice, thicken it with brown butter and Squeese on it a Lemon.

A white Fricasse of y Same.

Cut them in pieces & wash them from y blood & fry them on a soft fire then put them in a tossing pan with a little strong broth: season them & toss them up with mushrooms & oysters; w.^{n} almost enough put to them a pint of cream & thicken it with a bit of butter rould up in flower.

A Fricasse of Lamb.

Cut an hind quarter of lamb into thin Slices, Season it with Savoury Spice, Sweetherbs and a shallot then fry them & toss them up in strong broth, whitewine, oysters, balls & pallats, a little brown butter to thicken it or a bit of butter roul'd up in flower.

Pullets a la Cream.

Lard & force your Pullets of their own flesh boyld ham, mushrooms, sweetbreads, oysters, anchovys, grated bread y yolk of an egg, a little cream, spice & herbs, y^n roast y^m & pour on them a fine white ragooe of mushrooms, oysters sweetbreads, cocks combs, truffles, murrells & cream thicken d wth eggs.

G.1.

Kidder's Receipts.

Cutlets, A la Maintenoy.

Season your cutlets of mutton with Savoury Spice and shread sweet herbs: then dip 2 Scotch collops in $\bar{y}$ batter of eggs and clap on each side of each cutlet, & then a rasher of bacon on each side, broyl them upon paper, or bring them off in the oven, when they are dress't take off the bacon and send them up in a ragooe, and garnish them w.th slic'd orange & lemon.

A Leg of Lamb Forc'd.

Take the meat out of the leg close to the skin & bone and mince it with beef suet, thyme, parsley & onions, beat it in a mortar with Savoury spice and 2 anchovies: then wash the inside of the skin with $\bar{y}$ batter of eggs and fill it, bast flower & bake it: the Sauce may be season'd gravy, OR put to it a regalia of concumbers, colliflowers or french-beans.

To Roul a Breast of Veal or Mutton.

Bone your meat and make a savoury forc'd meat for it, wash it over with the batter of eggs: $\bar{y}$ⁿ spread the forc'd meat on it, roul it in a collar and bind it with pack-thread & roast it: put under it a regalia of concumber.

Pidgeons in Surtout.

Cleanse your pidgeons, then make a forceing for $\bar{y}$^m tye a large Scotch collop.& a Rasher of bacon on $\bar{y}$ breast of each: spit and cover them with paper & roast them then make for them a ragooe, and garnish them wth. Slic'd lemon.

G.2.

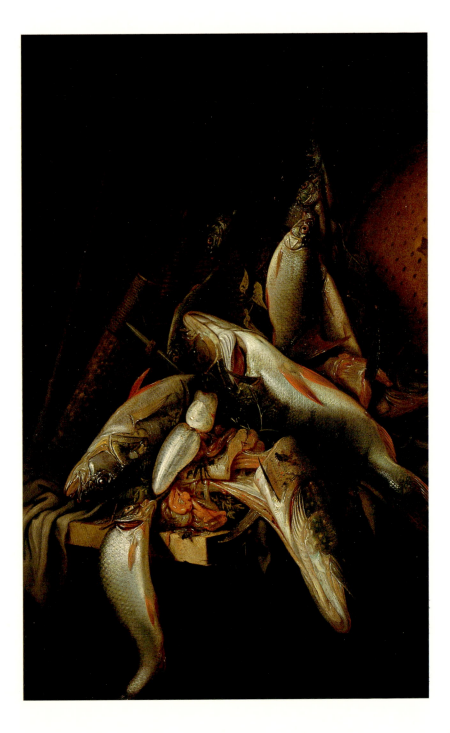

To Dress Fish

Kidders Receipts.

12

To Dress Fish
To Boyle a Cods-head

Set a kettle on the fire with water, vineager & Salt,
a faggot of Sweetherbs & an Onion or two; when the
liquor boyl'd put in the head on a fish bottom, and
in the boyling put in cold water & vineager, when it
is boyld take it up & put it in a dish that fits your
fish bottom; for the Sauce take gravy & clarret boyl'd
up with a faggot of Sweet-herbs & an Onion; 2 or 3
anchovys drawn up with 2 pound of butter a pint
of Shrimps oyst.rs y.e meat of a Lobster shred fine y.n put
the Sauce in Silver or China Basons, stick Small
toast on the head, lay on and about it the Spaune
milt & liver, garnish it with fry'd Parsley, Sliced
Lemon, Barberries & horse-radish. and fryed fish

To stew a Carp.

Take a Brace of Carp knock them on the head open
the bellies & wash out the blood with vineager & Salt,
then cut them close to the tail to the bone & wash them
clean, put them in a broad Sauce pan & put thereto a
quart of Clarret, half a pint of vineager a pint
of water, a faggot of Sweet herbs, a Nutmeg Sliced
large Mace, 4 or 5 Cloves, 2 or 3 racers of Ginger
whole pepper & and an Anchovy, cover them close
& Stew them a quarter of an hour then put to it the
blood and Vineager, and a bit of butter rold up in
flower lay about it the Spaune, milt & liver, stick on
them toasts thicken it with brown butter.

H.

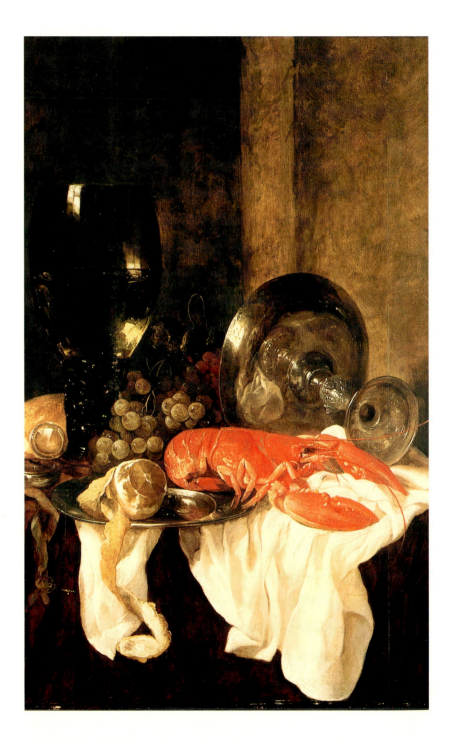

Kidders Receipts.

A Carp Larded w.th Eel in a Ragove.

Take a live carp knock him on the head, Scale and Slice him from head to tail in 4 or 5 Slices on the one Side to the bone: then take a good Silver eel and cut it as for larding as long and as thick as your little finger, rould in Spice and Sweetherbs and bay leaves powdered then lard it thick on the Slash'd Side fry it in a good pan of lard: then make for it a ragove with gravy, white wine vineager, clarret, the Spaune, mushrooms balls, capers, grated nutmeg, mace, a little pepper & Salt thicken it with brown butter and garnish it with Sliced lemon.

To Roast a Pike

Scale and slash a pike from head to tail and lard it with eels flesh rould in Sweet herbs & Spice and fill it with fish, forc'd meat, roast it at length bast and bread it: or you may turn his tail into his mouth and bring it off in the oven, let the Sauce be drawn butter, Anchovies, the row and liver with balls mushrooms, capers and Oysters and garnish it with Slic'd lemon

To Butter Lobsters.

Take out the meat and put it in a sauce pan with a little Season'd gravy and put to it a nutmeg a little vinegar and drawn butter, fill the Shells & Set the rest in plates. Forc'd Eel Mince it w.th Oysters, sweet herbs Onions suet bread & egg, fill y Skin turn it round, & bake or broyl it drawn butter & lemon H.1.

Potting & Pasties

Kidders Receipts.

13

Potting.

To Pott Beef.

Take a good buttock of beef or leg of mutton piece, cut it in pieces and season it with Savoury Spice an ounce of Salt peter ½ a pint of Clarret, then let it lye all night: then put it in a pan and lay over it 3 or 4 pound of butter, tye a paper over it and bake it with houshold bread: then take it out and dry it in a cloth and beat it in a mortar very fine; then pour to it the butter clear from the gravy and mix it together then put it close in potts, Set it in the oven to Settle: when it is cold cover it with clarrified butter.

To Pott Pidgeons.

Your pidgeons being trust & season'd with Savoury Spice, put them in a pot, cover them with butter & bake them, then take them out & drain them, when cold cover them w.th clarryfide butter. You may pot fish the same way: but let them be bone'd when they are bak'd.

Pasties. A Venison Pasty.

Bone a side or haunch of venison, cut it square & Season it with pepper & Salt, make it up in yo.r aforesaid pasty past: a peck of flower for a buk pasty & 3 quar.rs for a doc, 2 pound of butter at y bottom of yo.r buck pasty & a p.d & ½ for a doe.

A Lamb Pasty is made as the Doe.

A Beef Pasty so cut out & season'd over night with pepper, Salt, a little red wine & Cochineel: Then made up as the Buck Pasty.

To each of these Pasties pour in a Lear.

I.

Collaring

Kidders Receipts. 14

Collaring
To Collar Beef.

Lay your Flank of Beef in Ham brine 8 or 10
days, then dry it in a cloth and take out all the lea
ther and Skin Scotch it cross and Season it with
Savoury Spice, 2 or 3 anchovys an handfull or
two of thyme Sweet marjoram winter Savoury
and Onions, Strew it on the meat and roul it
in a hard collar in a cloth. Sew it close & tye
it at both ends and put it in a collar pot with a
pint of Clarret and Cochineel and two quarts
of pump water and bake it all night: then take it
out hot and tye it close at both ends: then set it up on
one end and put a weight upon it and let it stand till
it is cold: then take it out of the cloth and keep it dry

To Collar Eeles.

Scover ye large Silver eeles with Salt, Slit y^m down
the back, take out the bones wash & dry them & Season y^m
with Savoury Spice, minc'd parsley, thyme, Sage and an
onion then roul each in collars, in a little cloth, tye them
close and boyl them in water & Salt wth ye heads & bones
& ½ a pint of vineager a faggot of herbs ginger a pennyworth of iccinglass, when they are tender take y^m up tye
them close again Strain ye pickle & keep the Eeles in it.

I.1.

Kidders Receipts.

To Collar Veal.

Bone a breast of Veal wash and Soake it in 3 or
4 waters, dry it in a cloth and Season it with savoury
Spice Shread Sweet-herbs and rashers of Bacon,
dipt in the batter of eggs and roul them up in a collar
in a cloth and boyl it in water and Salt with ½ a
pint of vineager and whole Spice Scum it clean
when it is boyl'd take it up and when cold keep it
in this Pickle

To Collar Pig

Slit the Pig down the back take out all the bones
wash out the blood in 3 or 4 waters, wipe it dry,
and Season it with Savoury Spice, thyme parsley &
Salt and roul it in a hard collar, tye it close in a dry
cloth and boyl it with the bones in 3 pints of water,
a handfull of Salt, a quart of vineager, a faggot of
Sweet-herbs, whole Spice a pennyworth of Iceing
glass when it is boyl'd tender take it off and when cold
take it out of the cloth & keep it in this pickle.

To Collar Pork.

Bone a breast of pork Season it with Savoury
Spice & a good quantity of Sage, parsley & thyme
roul it in an hard collar in a cloth tye it close and
boyle it when its cold keep it in Sousing drink.

I.2.

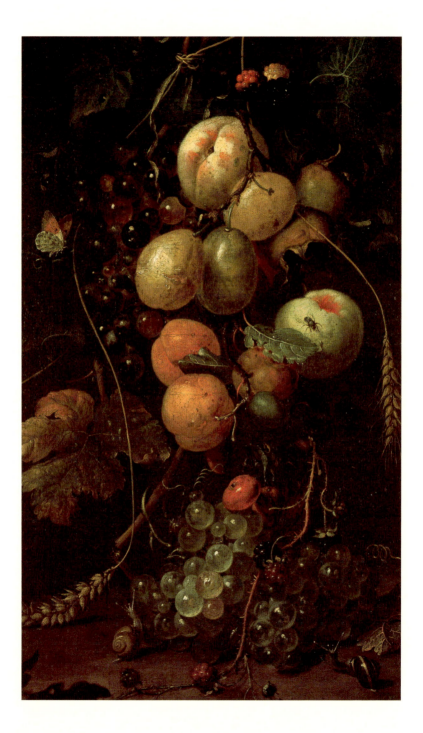

Pickles

Kidders Reciepts.

Pickles.

To Pickle Mellons or large Cowcumbers.

Scoop them at one end and take out the pulp clean, and fill them with Scrap'd horse-raddish, Slic'd garlick, ginger, nutmeg, whole pepper and large mace; then for the pickle: The best white-wine vineager, an handfull of Salt, a quarter'd nutmeg, whole pepp^r, cloves and mace and 2 or 3 racers of ginger boyl'd all together. And pour it to the Mellons boyling hot & Stow them down close 2 days; when you intend to green them, Set them over the fire in a bell-mettle pot in their pickle till they are Scalding hot and green then pour them into your pots, Stow them down close: when cold cover them with a wet bladder and leather. Thus cover all other pickles.

To Pickle Gerkin Cowcumbers.

Put them in a brine 2 or 3 days Strong enough to bear an egg; then drain them from the brine and pour on them the Same pickle as the Mellons boyling hot and green them and cover them as before.

To Pickle French Beans.

Put them a month in brine strong enough to bear an egg; then drain them from the brine and pour on them ye same pickle as the Mellons boyling hot & green them the Same way

K.

Kidders Receipts.

To Pickle Wallnuts.

Scal'd them and put them into water & salt for 9 or 10 days, changing it every day, then take them out & rub them with a course cloth & pour on them y̌ same pickle as the mellons, adding thereto a little mustard Seed.

To Pickle Mushrooms.

Take your Small hard buttons, cut y̌ dirt from y̌ bottom of the Stalks, wash them with water & rub them very clean with flannell, then boyl water & Salt; when it boyls throw in your mushrooms & when they are boyl'd quick & white, Strain them thro a cloth, then throw them into cold water & Salt for 2 or 3 days, changing it twice a day, then let the pickle be white wine vineager with Slic'd nutmeg, ginger, pepper, cloves & mace then stop y̌ᵐ up in glasses.

To Pickle Onions.

Boyle your small white onions in water & Salt, Strain and cool them in a cloth, then let the Pickle be Vineager and Spice cold as the Mushrooms. *Good*

Collyflowers may be done y̌ Same way.

To Pickle Beat Roots & Turnips.

Boyl your Beat Root in water & Salt, a pint of vineager, a little Cochineal, when they are half boyl'd put in y̌ Turnips being pare'd, when they are boil'd take them off the fire & keep them in this pickle.

To Pickle Red Cabbage.

Slice the Cabbage thinn and put to it a pickle of vineager & Spice cold.

K.1.

Kidder's Receipts.

Barberries are pickl'd only in strong Brine of water & Salt. *To Pickle Aristacon flowers*

or Clove Gilly Flowers.

Pickle them in half white wine & half Vineager & Sugar when boyl'd & cold.

To Pickle Pidgeons.

Boyl them w.th whole Spice, in 3 p.ts of water, a p. of white wine, & a p.t of vineager; when boyl'd take them up, & when cold keep them in this pickle.

To Pickle Smelts.

Lay y.m in a pot in rows, lay on y.m slic'd Lemon, ginger, nutmeg, mace, pepper & bay leaves powder'd, & Salt, let y. pickle be red wine vineager, bruis'd Cochinele & peter salt, let y. pickle be boyl'd & cold & pour'd on y.m & Cover y.m close. To Pickle Oysters.

Take a q.rt of large Oysters in y. full of y. moon, parboyl'd in y. own liq.r for y. pickle, take y. liq.r a p.nt of white wine & vineager, mace, pepper & salt, boyl & Scum it, w.n cold keep the Oysters in this pickle.

To Stew Mushrooms. Peel &

beard yo.r flaps & boyl y.m in water & Salt strain y.m & stew y.m in a little of y. liq.r a little white wine, savoury spice & lemon thicken it w.th a bit of butter roull'd up in flower.

Catchup of Mushrooms. Stew yo.r fresh flaps in y. own liq. Oyster liq.r white wine, anchovys, spice, shallots, sweet herbs, boyl & strain it, & keep it in bottles.

K 2

Jellies

Kidder's Receipts. 16

Jellies.

Harts-horn Jelly.

Put ½ a pound of harts-horn into an earthen-pan with 2 quarts of Spring water, cover it close & set it in the oven all night, then Strain it into a clean pipkin with ½ a pint of rhennish wine and ½ a pound of double refin'd Sugar, the juice of 3 or 4 lemons, 3 or 4 blades of mace and the whites of 4 or 5 eggs well beat and mix it that it curdle not Set it on the fire and Stir it well together then let it Stand over the fire till it a-riseth with a thick Skum, run it thro' a napkin and turn it up again till it is all clear.

Calves feet Jelley

Boyl a pair of Calves feet in water with ye meat cut off from the bones, when cold take the fatt from ye top and ye dross from ye bottom and Season it as ye Harts-horn jelley.

Riban Jelley.

Is made with ye colour'd jelleys hereafter mention'd First run one of those colours in a glass, n^n it is cold, run another as cold as you can & y^n another & so all ye rest.

To run Colours.

Have in yor Severall small pipkins strong jel-lies ready season'd have also several muslin rags ty'd up close one wth bruis'd cochineal, another wth Saffron & another wth Spinnage juice put yor bags into yor Several pipkins, & as you would y^e colours rise fine y^m with the whites of eggs, & run them thro' Several bags.

L.

Kidder's Receipts.

Blamangoes.

Make your jelly of ½ of harts horn and 2 q.^rts of Spring water, run it thrô a napkin, put to it ½ a pound of jordan almonds well beat, mix with it orange flower water, a pint of milk or cream the juice of 2 or 3 lemon and double refin'd Sugar, let it simmer over the fire and take care least it burn too run it thrô a Sive 2 or 3 times colour it if you please and put it in glasses.

A whipt Sillabub.

Take a pint of cream with a little orange flower water, 2 or 3 ounce' of fine Sugar, the juice of a lemon, the white of 3 eggs: whisk these up light together and having in your glasses rhennish wine and Sugar and clarret & Sugar, lay on the froth wth a Spoon heap'd up as high as you can.

A Sack Posset.

Take 14 eggs, leave out half of the whites & beat them with a quarter of a pound of white sugar oringoe roots slic'd very then with a quarter of a pint of Sack, mix it well together; Set it on the fire and keep Stirring it all one way: when it is scalding hott let another whilst you stirr it, pour into it q.^rt of cream boiling hot with a grated nutmeg boil'd in it: Then take it off the fire, clap a hot pye plate on it and let it stand a quarter of an hour.

Orange Butter

Take ye yolks of 3 hard eggs, a pound of butter, a little fine Sugar e'a spoonsfull of orange flower water & work it thrô a Sive Almond & Pistachia butter is made y.^e same way only blanch & pound them.

L.1.

Lemon Cream.

Take the juice of 3 or 4 Lemons & boyl some of
the peel in spring water then take double the quantity of that water as Lemon juice then put to it orange
flower water & $\frac{1}{2}$ a pound of double refin'd sugar y^n
beat the whites of 12 eggs & strain them y mix them
together & keep it stirring over a charcoal fire till
tis pritty thick y^n put it in glasses. Orange Cream it
made the same way only thickned with yolks of
eggs instead of whites.

Snow Cream.

Take a pint of Cream the whites of 4 eggs fine sugar
& a little hony water wisk it up in a broad earthen
pan & take of the froth as it ariseth.

Rasberry Cream.

Take a quart of custard stuff & mix it wth bruis'd
ripe rasberries or preserv'd ones gather it over y
fire & strain it then put it in glasses. Thus you may
make any other sort of Cream wth altering the fruit.

Chocolate Cream.

Take a pint of Cream wth a spoonfull of scrapt
Chocolate boyl it well together mix wth it y^e yolks
of 2 eggs & thicken & mill it on the fire y^n
put it in glasses.

Italian Cream & Sugar Loaß.

Take a q^t of strong jelly run & mix it w^{th} $\frac{1}{2}$ a
pound of Almonds well pounded pouring to it in
pounding Cream, strain it 2 or 3 times y warm
all together & when half cold fill a bason & jelly
glaßes when cold dip your bason & glaßes in hot
water to loosen them & turn them in china plates.

L. 2.

Kidders Receipts.

To Coddle Codlings.

Put your fair Codlings in a brass pan w.th
water over a charcole fire till it is Scalding hott
keep them close cover'd, when they will Skin then
Skin them and put them in again with a little vin
eager and let them lye till they are green

To Bottle Goosberries etc.

When they are full grown, before they turn, fill
them into wide mouth'd bottles, cork them closs, and
Sett them in a slack oven till they are tender and
crackt, then take them out & pitch y corks.

Thus you may keep,

Damsons Bullace

Pears Plums or

Currants &c.

Only do these when they are ripe.

To Salt Hams or Tongues

Take 3 or 4 gallons of water, put to it 4 pound of
bay Salt 1 pound of white Salt, a pound of petre salt
a quarter of a pound of Salt petre, 2 ounces of pra-
nella Salt & a pound of brown Sugar let it boil a
quarter of an hour, Scum it well, when it is cold
Sever it from the bottom into the vessel you keep
it in

Let Hams lye in this pickle 4 or 5 weeks

A Clod of Dutch Beef as long

Tongues a forthnight

Collar'd Beeff 8 or 10 days

Dry them in a Stove or w.th n ood in a Chimney.

L.3.

First Dishes.
1

Pottages of all Sorts.
A Dish of Fish.
Beans and Bacon.
A Ham *and* Chickens.
Pullets and Oysters.
Boyl'd Tongues & Udders.
A Leg of Veal, Bacon & herbs
A Calves head Bacon & hebs
A Neck of Veal Bacon herbs
A Calves head hash'd.
A Goose or Turkey a la Daub.
A Leg of Veal or Mutton, a la Daub.
A Bisk of Pidgeons.
A forc'd Leg of Veal boyl'd.
A Powder'd Haunch of Venison.
A Powder'd Leg of Pork.
A Leg of Mutton and Turnips.
A piece of salt Beef and Carrots.
Pullets Bacon & Cabbage
Boyl'd Fowls & marrow Bones.
A Turbut & Small fish.
A Ham or red tongues w.th Chickens or Pidgeons n.th
Herbs forc'd or plain
A Boyl'd Turkey & Oysters.
Stew'd Giblets.
A Leg of Lamb & Spinnage or goosberries.
Boyl'd Rabbits.

MIDDLE DISHES.
2

A grand Sallad of Pickles.
A hot or cold Pye.
Tarts Cheescakes.

Puffs & custards.
Jellies, Creams & Blamangoes. A Dish of Fruit
A Sweet-meat Tart.
A Patty of Lobsters.
Cold Lobsters.
Puddings.

BOTTOM DISHES.
3

A Chine of Veal or Mutton,
A Gigot of mutton.
A neck of Veal. Pidgeons in Surtout Puddings of any sort. Roast Beef.
minc'd Pyes. Cold Ham
Slic'd tongue. A Venison Pasty. Potted meats or Fowls. Cold Lobster.
Salmon or Sturgeon.
A haunch of Venison roast a Leg of mutton roast n.th Oysters. Lamb in Joynts.
A Chine & Turkey. Chickens or Pidgeons roast n.th
Asparagus, Pullets or Turkey n.th eggs. A Roast Pike.
a Calves head roasted Pidgeon pears. Bombarded-Veal. Roast Turkey or Fowls n.th Sausages.

SIDE DISHES.
4

Bombarded Veal.
Scotch'd Collops.
A forc'd leg of Lamb.
Cutlets a la Maintenoy.
Cutlets forc'd.
Fricassies white or brown
A Ragooe of any sort.
a Tourt or Tansie. Peas,
Beans or French-beans.
Scollop'd Oysters.
Olives of Veal.
Carp in a Ragooe.

Chickens & Asparagus.
Lamb-stones & Sweetbreads
Stew'd or forc'd Carp.
Chickens a la Creame.
A Pompetone.

Second Course.
5

A dish of wild or tame Fowl of any sort. Rabbits,
Ducklings, Green Geese or Pidgeons, Turkey Pouts,
Leverets, Partridges.
Woodcocks or Snips.
Pheasants, Quails Larks
Wheat-ears, Ducks Widgeons, Plovers.
A Comport of Pidgeons
Pidgeons broild or Stew'd
Butter'd Lobsters or Crabs
Artichokes boyld
Asparagus & eggs.
Schollop'd Oysters.
Pitty Patties.
A Tourt or Tansy.
Tarts, Cheese-cakes,
Puffs & Custards.
A Dish of Peas.
A Ragooe of Mushrooms
A Ragooe of any sort.
Lobsters Ragoo'd or Roast.
A Pompetone.
Oyster Loaves.
Tourts of Marrow or Cream
Veal Cutletts.
Olives of Veal.
Patties of Oysters.
Craw-fish Prawns, Shrimps
Fitters of Abricocks or
Oysters.
Polonia Sausages.
Slic'd Tongue.
Solomon gundy.
Potting Collaring or Pickles of any sort.

Index

Kidder's Minc'd Pyes.

Pear Pye high.
Apple Pye low.

Kidder's Minc'd Pyes.

Neats Tongue Pye.

Lamb or Veal Pye.

Set Custards.

Egg Pyes.

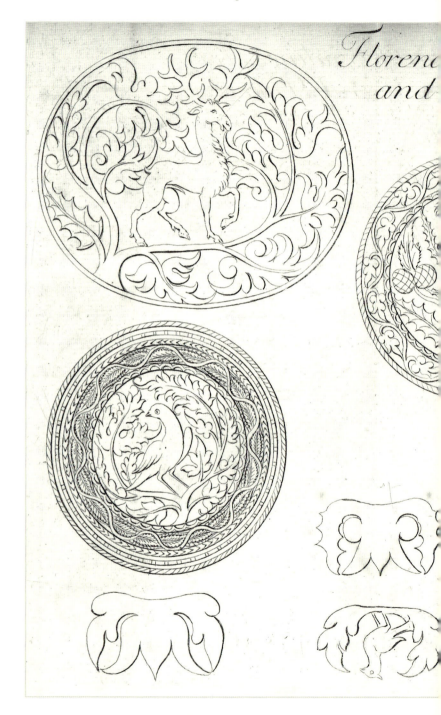

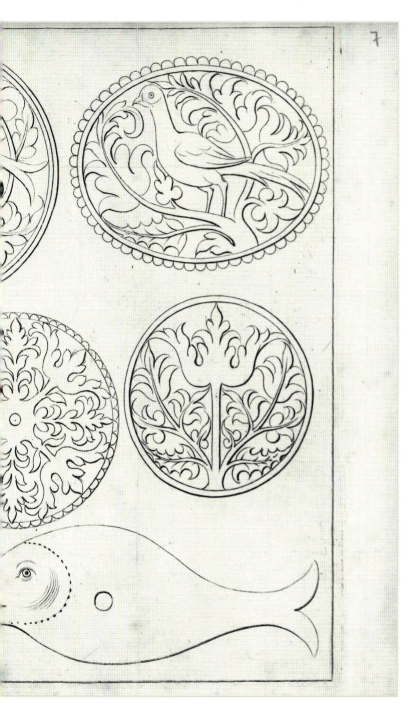

Swan, Turky or Goose Pye

Pid

Hare or Rabbet Pye

Lumber Pye

Pye

Wild Fowl Pye

Pye

Giblet Hen or Mutton Pye

Calves Head Pye

Pye

Select Bibliography

Aylmer, Ursula, ed. *Oxford Food, an Anthology*. Ashmolean Museum and Bodleian Library Publications, 1995

Davidson, Alan. *The Oxford Companion to Food*. OUP, 1999

Driver, Christopher, ed. *John Evelyn, Cook*. Prospect Books, 1997

Feild, Rachel. *Irons in the Fire*. Crowood Press, 1984

Glasse, Hannah. *The Art of Cookery made Plain and Easy* [facsimile ed.]. Prospect Books, 1983

Larousse Gastronomique [English ed.]. Hamlyn, 1961

May, Robert. *The Accomplish't Cook,* [facsimile ed.]. Prospect Books, 1999

Midgley, Graham. *University Life in Eighteenth-Century Oxford*. Yale University Press, 1996

Potter, David. Some notes on Edward Kidder. *Petits Propos Culinaires*, 65, pp. 9–11. Prospect Books, 2000.

Quayle, Eric. *Old Cook Books, An Illustrated History*. Studio Vista, 1978

Schoonover, David E., ed. Edward Kidder: *Receipts of Pastry and Cookery for the Use of his Scholars*. University of Iowa, 1993 [Edition of the manuscript in the Száthmary Collection, University of Iowa]

GLOSSARY

Abricocks Apricots

Ala daub [= À la daube] Braised in the oven in a rich wine stock.

A la Maintenoy [= À la Maintenon?] According to the 'Larousse Gastronomique', À la Maintenon implies the addition of mushrooms or truffles and sometimes pickled tongue to a sauce or mixture, but this appears to be a quite different recipe. Madame de Maintenon, 1635–1719, was the mistress, and possibly the second wife, of Louis XIV and her name, or an approximation of it, would add a note of high French fashion to a menu.

Aristacon Flowers Carnations, see *Clove Gilly Flowers.*

Barberries Sharp-flavoured red berries from a shrub of the berberis variety. Redcurrants would be a modern substitute.

Battalia Meats of small farmyard creatures such as poultry and young rabbits. The word comes from the French 'bétail', meaning cattle. The 'Larousse Gastronomique' complains of its erroneous use to mean small livestock, which is evidently the usage here.

Bay Salt Sea salt, especially that imported in Kidder's day from Bourgneuf Bay at the mouth of the Loire.

Blamangoes Blancmange

Bombarded Formed into shape by a bomb-shaped mould.

Bullace Wild plum

Catsup, Catchup Ketchup. The presence of anchovies in the sauce indicates a great antiquity for this recipe, and the probable descent of the sauce from 'Garum', the ubiquitous salty fish-flavoured relish and cooking medium of ancient Rome.

Caudle A thick spicy drink made by thickening wine or ale with breadcrumbs, egg-yolks etc, considered very nourishing for invalids.

Caul Sheet of fat surrounding the intestines.

Cheese Cakes The recipe given here is for the filling only. Cottage cheese can be substituted for the curds made from the milk. If scaling this recipe down, the proportion would be half a cup of cottage cheese to 1 cup of cream.

Clod Large piece

Clove Gilly Flowers Pinks or Carnations [= *Aristacon Flowers*], pickled to add a faintly clove-like flavour.

Coddle To boil very gently

Codlings A type of apple: Hot Codlings were roasted apples sold in the London streets.

Collops Slices or pieces of meat.

Collar Meat or fish cooked or cured in a roll of cloth fastened so that it formed a circle.

Comport = Compôte. This is usually used today to describe a sweet fruit-based preparation, but the 'Larousse Gastronomique' notes that the word is also used for certain dishes of pigeons or partridges which have had long cooking. This was evidently the meaning in Kidder's day.

Crag Neck of mutton or veal.

Cream/Creme Kidder's recipe for Custard allows for cream or milk to be used. However, in modern dairy-making the separation of cream from milk is so efficient that it is quite difficult to thicken mixtures if milk is used. Where an old recipe allows a choice, it is probably always better to opt for cream.

Custard At this period a pudding in its own right rather than a sweet sauce. Kidder's instruction 'then fill your custard being dry'd in the oven' probably means 'fill the dish or pastry case and cook till the custard is set.' 'The Oxford Companion to Food' notes that custard was often cooked in bread-ovens which had cooled after the loaves had been taken out. John Evelyn, in the second half of the seventeenth century, gives a recipe which instructs baking a custard for quarter of an hour with the lid on the dish and a further quarter of an hour with the lid removed. Where the quantity is based on a pint of cream or milk, modern recipe books recommend cooking in a dish for 30–40 minutes, or till set, in a low oven. The dish should preferably be put in a bain-marie to prevent burning.

See also the note under *Cream.*

Drawn [of butter]. As a substitute for a roux, to make a liaison for thickening a sauce, butter can be broken into small pieces and worked into flour before it is added to the dish; it absorbs about its own weight. Because butter contained many impurities, it was necessary to be very careful when melting it for cooking to avoid having burnt bits. Hannah Glasse instructed the cook to add a spoonful of cold water and a dusting of flour and to use a silver pan.

Florendine Shallow round pie made with very thin pastry.

Forc'd, Forced Stuffed

Gallendine Not our modern 'Galantine' a dish served cold in aspic jelly, but a sauce for venison made by boiling claret, spices and sugar. It was used in this sense by John Evelyn in the seventeenth century.

Hart's Horn, Hartshorn Shavings from a stag's antlers. Gelatine is the modern substitute.

Heart Pans Patty pans shaped in the form of hearts.

High Pye Raised pie on a flat base, as distinct from one in a dish.

Humble Pye Pie made from the intestines of deer, etc.

Iceingglass, Isinglass A substance made from the swimming-bladders of some fish such as the sturgeon. It was the successor of hartshorn and predecessor of gelatine in setting jellies, etc.

Lamb Stones Lambs' testicles

Larded Threaded through with strips of fat or fatty bacon in order to keep the meat moist while cooking. Where large fish such as carp and pike are concerned, Kidder's instructions are to use strips of eel, suitable because eel is very oily and would also enhance the fishy flavour.

Lear A thickening or binding sauce or savoury jelly, poured into a pie to hold the contents in firm shape. [Fr. 'Lier', to bind]. Kidder seems to have remembered to add the word to some of his recipes at the last minute [eg *A Calves Head Pye* on p. 29] which vividly evokes the cook rushing to add the 'lear' at the last moment.

Lumber Pie Perhaps derived from Lombard. Mrs. Beeton gives a recipe for 'Lombard Soup' which, like Kidder's 'Pye', contains spinach and other greenstuff as well as suet and meat. The well-travelled merchants of Lombardy had strong cultural influences on other countries and their wealth ensured an elaborate cuisine.

Mill To whisk

Moy Bone Marrow [Fr. 'Moelle'].

Murrells = Morels, fine-flavoured type of mushroom.

Neat Bovine animal, such as ox or cow.

Orange Flower Water A flavouring prepared from distilled orange blossom, which reached Europe from the Middle East via Sicily, Spain and Portugal. It is still obtainable from specialist shops, but when buying it mention that it is needed for cooking: there is a variety made for cosmetic purposes which is for external application.
Oringoe = Eringo Root. The root of the sea-holly, usually eaten preserved in sugar or pickled. Candied chestnuts might be the closest modern substitute as far as flavour is concerned, but eringo was believed to be an aphrodisiac and may have originally featured in recipes for this reason.

Pallets Palates, see also *Shiver'd Pallets*.

Paste Pastry

Peck A stone [14 pounds, approx. 6.5 kilos] in weight; half a gallon in traditional dry measurement system used for cereals, etc.

Penny loaf A plain penny loaf was made with coarse flour and weighed about 12ozs–1lb. A penny white loaf, as in Kidder's recipe for 'Lumber Pie', was half that size but of better quality, made with fine flour, milk and eggs. Elizabeth David's 'English Bread and Yeast Cookery', [Penguin, 1987], gives details.

Petre salt, saltpetre Petre salt was nitre, called saltpetre when it had been refined. See also *Prunella Salt*. Nitrates were used in preserving to give a good red colour. The Prospect edition, 1983, of Hannah Glasse's cookery book, has a learned and comprehensive note on the subject in the Glossary [p. 197], which also discusses Dr. Johnson's definition.

Pipkin Round pot, usually of earthenware, which could be used for cooking.

Pippins Apples, especially the dessert varieties.

Pompetone A pie where a rolled-out stuffing mixture was used instead of pastry. David Schoonover, the editor of the Iowa manuscript, reads this as 'Porpetone' and sees it as a version of the 'Porpentine' or 'Porcupine' recipe given by May, where the dish is stuck over with almonds [= quills] before serving. But this method of presentation is not mentioned at all by Kidder.

Posset Drink made by adding wine, spices, etc. to lightly curdled milk or cream which developed into a sweet similar to a syllabub, etc.

Powder'd Scattered with garnishes or dredged with spices.

Pruants Prunes

Prunellas Sloes [French, 'Prunelles']

Prunella Salt Nitrate made into small cakes or balls . See also *Petre Salt.*

Quart 2 pints, just over a litre.

Ragoo[= Ragôut] A thick, rich stew.

Regalia Garnish, decoration.

Rillet There is a preparation known as 'Rillettes' which consists of diced pork or fish, seasoned, cooked and cooled, but 'rillet' here simply seems to be a mistake for 'fillet'.

Sack Fortified white wine, esp. sherry, imported from Spain or the Canaries.

Savoury Balls Small meat and suet dumplings. Fish balls were another version. These were the equivalent of our stock cubes, added to give body and flavour to sauces and gravies. See also *Sweet Balls*

Savoury Pies, Sweet Pies Whether these were classified as sweet or savoury depended on the nature of the spices, sauces, etc., rather than on the main ingredients. Thus meat could be a constituent of a 'sweet' pie.

Savoury Spice, Sweet Spice – 'Sweet Spice is Cloves, Mace, Nutmeg, Cinnamon and Salt if for meat pyes Fowls or Fish with a little fine pepper. Savoury Spice is Pepper, Salt, Cloves, Mace and Nutmeg'.

Schum Skim

Scotcht, Scored Gashed. In the recipe for Scotch Collops, 'scotch them with the back of a knife' probably corresponds to an instruction in the cookery book of Ralph Ayres to hack beef steak with the back of a cleaver. It meant to tenderise meat by beating it. We would now use a cook's mallet or tenderiser for the purpose.

Scrap't Grated

Shiver'd Pallets Palate of beef was frequently eaten at this time. Instructions are usually given to boil it till tender before adding it to other dishes. 'To shiver' meant to shred or break up, as in 'Shiver my timbers'.

Skerret, Skirret Type of parsnip. It is an indication of the long history of this recipe that Kidder gives it as an alternative to the potato, a century and a half after potatoes arrived in Britain.

Solomon Gundy Salmagundy, Salmagundi. A substantial salad with cold meats and eggs. Great care was taken to lay out the ingredients to make an attractive dish.

Spanish Potatoes Sweet potatoes, brought back by the Spaniards from the Americas and grown in southern Spain.

Spit it between 8 squers [as in the recipe for fillet of beef, p. 59]. This can probably be interpreted as 'cut it into 8 pieces and cook them on a spit'. Rachel Feild in 'Irons in the Fire' comments that in the eighteenth century 'the Englishman remained wedded to the spit ...' [p.64]. Roasting was a very uneven process unless a spit was used and an expensive and delicate piece of meat such as a whole fillet could be easily ruined.

Spoonful This seems to have implied an implement much larger than our tablespoon or dessertspoon, more in the nature of a cook's ladle. In testing the recipe for Chocolate Cream, I found that 50 grams of grated chocolate was about right as Kidder's 'spoonful'.

Sugar sack In the recipe for Custard, p. 39, this should probably read 'sugar, sack', implying these should be added to taste. John Farley's recipe book of 1783 recommends adding to the cream and eggs 'a little rose and orange-flower water and sack, and nutmeg and sugar to your palate'. The usual amount of sugar to add to a pint of cream is 2oz, 70 grams. For the 'sack', add a tablespoon of sherry if liked.

Surtout A covering, meaning also in Kiddder's time a coat or hooded cloak [from the French, meaning 'Over everything'].

Sweet Balls Small meat and suet dumplings with currants, lemon peel, etc. added.

Sweetbread Pancreas

Tort Tart

Tansey, tansy Herb with a spicy scent used in both sweet and sour dishes. It gave its name to a cream pudding.

Umbles Intestines, sometimes used more generally to include liver, heart and other offal.

Wiggs A Lent speciality, small cakes, originally made from a round cake cut into wedges; they were served with mulled wine instead of mince pies, or for breakfast. Ralph Ayres, the eighteenth-century cook at New College, gives a recipe for 'London Wiggs', so they were evidently considered a metropolitan sophistication in some quarters.

Win[d]sor Beans Broad Beans

Verjuice Acid juice of sour or unripe fruit. Lemon juice or wine vinegar are modern substitutes.

INDEX OF RECIPE TITLES

The spelling has occasionally been modernised to make the Index easier to use.

INDEX OF COLOUR ILLUSTRATIONS

All the colour illustrations consist of details taken from pictures in the Ashmolean Museum's Ward Collection of 17th century Dutch and Flemish still-life paintings and include works by: